Cinderella

Kaye Umansky

Illustrated by Caroline Crossland

A & C BLACK • LONDON

Contents

A Letter from the Playwright

During my fourteen hair-raising years teaching in primary schools, it frequently fell to my lot to organise The Play. Usually, because I was keen (well, I always was at the beginning!) the productions tended to be ambitious, involving the whole school and taking up half a term. Not everyone had a speaking part, of course - but somehow we managed to involve everybody in some capacity - either in the choir, or the orchestra, or in the stage management team, designing the scenery or making props and costumes. It's amazing how many people you can fit in!

However, I hope you will use this play in any way that you want to, either to put on a full production, or to act or read some scenes from it in the classroom. If you decide to do the latter, I would like to offer one word of advice and suggest that you talk to the children about reading a play, and how it differs from reading a story. You could tell the children about the characters in the play (see pages 42 - 43) and introduce them to the idea of speaking dialogue in character. You could explain that, although it might sound obvious, the humorous lines should sound funny! You could also give them an idea of what pace and timing are. Some time spent in preparation will enable them to get a lot more from the experience.

All schools have different facilities, and whether you decide to read scenes from *Cinderella*, or stage the play for production, you will need to adapt it to suit your circumstances. A friend and fellow teacher has recently produced the play at her school. She found that she needed to expand the number of speaking parts. Her ingenious solution was to divide up Gary the Guard's lines and introduce a whole troup of guards - Gary, Harry, Barry and Larry! On the other hand, some children may prefer a non-speaking role, in which case you can easily enlarge the number of mice in order to include them in the cast. I hope the 'Director's Notes' will prove helpful to you. But feel free to experiment, change and adapt. That's what theatre is all about.

Characters in Order of Appearance

The Mice: Main Mouse
       Skweek
       Tiptoe
       Longtail
       Wetnose
       Snitch
       (and as many more as you wish)
Grabber the Cat
Cinderella

Buttons
Semolina
Ravioli
Gary the Guard
Prince Charming
Old Woman/Fairy Godmother
Baron Hardup
Courtiers and Guests
Footman

List of Scenes and their Locations

Prologue - Mouse Talk   : *Front of stage area*

Act 1

Scene 1 - Poor Cinderella   : *The Kitchen*
Scene 2 - Rotten Relations   : *The Bedroom*
Scene 3 - Chance Meetings : *The Wood*
Scene 4 - Great News!   : *The Kitchen*

[Interval if desired]

Act 2

Scene 1 - The Transformation : *The Kitchen*
Scene 2 - Having a Ball!   : *The Palace Ballroom*
Scene 3 - The Shoe Fits   : *The Kitchen*
Scene 4 - Happy Ever After   : *Front of stage area*

The playing time is approximately 45 minutes without an interval.

Prologue – Mouse Talk

The Kitchen. Lights up. It is deserted. There is a table at the back of the stage with a large cheese displayed on it and a broom propped up against it. There is a chair drawn up to the table. CINDERELLA's shawl hangs from the back of the chair. Off stage, quiet at first then getting louder, we hear a rhythmic chant of "Cheese! Cheese! Cheese! Cheese!" Enter the MICE at the front of the stage.

ALL MICE: Cheese! Cheese!
Cheese! Cheese!
Something 'bout the smell that
Brings me to me knees!
Do we want some?
Ooh yes please!
'Cause nothing beats the pong
Of good strong cheese!

MAIN MOUSE: Do we want Cheshire?

ALL MICE: Yes, sir, yes, sir!

MAIN MOUSE: Do we want Cheddar?

ALL MICE: Nothing bedder!

MAIN MOUSE: Do we want Dutch?

ALL MICE: Ooh, not much!

MAIN MOUSE: What do we want, gang?

ALL MICE: <u>We want cheese!</u>

(With shrill squeaks, they converge excitedly upon the table.)

MAIN MOUSE: Wait a minute! Hold it right there!

(The MICE freeze, paws extended.)

SKWEEK: What's the problem, Main Mouse?

MAIN MOUSE: We're not just here to pinch cheese, you know.

ALL MICE: We're not?

MAIN MOUSE: Certainly not. We're here to tell the tale.

TIPTOE: Tail? Whose tail?

(They examine their tails puzzledly.)

MAIN MOUSE: Not <u>that</u> sort of tail, you ignorant lot! I'm talking about the <u>story</u>. How it all began. It's our job to fill in the background.

ALL MICE: It is?

MAIN MOUSE: Yep. In fact -

      We're here to fill the role
Of storyteller,
To tell about a girl
Called Cinderella.

SKWEEK: Got no one
To take her side
Ever since the
Poor girl's mother died...

TIPTOE: Leaving her alone
With her poor old dad.

ALL MICE: Ready with your hankies?
This gets sad.

MAIN MOUSE: Along comes a widow
With a big fat purse.
Dad gets married!
Things get worse...

LONGTAIL: Hold it, hold it. Things get <u>worse</u>?

MAIN MOUSE: Oh yes. Much worse.

LONGTAIL: But Cinderella's father became a rich Baron, didn't he?
                And they moved to Hardup Hall and everything.

MAIN MOUSE: True. But you're forgetting the stepsisters.
                Semolina and Ravioli. What a combination.
                They made Cinderella's life a misery.

LONGTAIL: Three boos for the nasty old stepsisters. Hip, hip...

ALL MICE: Booooooo!

LONGTAIL: Hip, hip...

ALL MICE: Booooooo!

LONGTAIL: Hip, hip...

ALL MICE: Booooooo!

WETNOSE: Is that it, then, Main Mouse? Have we finished
                filling in the background?

MAIN MOUSE: More or less.

WETNOSE: Good. Let's eat the cheese!

(Another rush at the table.)

MAIN MOUSE: Hold it!

SKWEEK: <u>Now</u> what?

MAIN MOUSE: I've been thinking. About all this cheese pinching we've
                been doing. I keep asking myself. Is it right?

TIPTOE: Ripe? Of course it's ripe. Lovely, that is, all oozy and smelly -

MAIN MOUSE: Not ripe, right! Is it right, I ask myself? Because you
                know what'll happen, don't you? If we pinch the cheese?

LONGTAIL: Well, we'll all get some lunch for a start...

MAIN MOUSE: Yes, but Cinderella will get into trouble again. And we all like Cinderella, don't we?

WETNOSE: True. She feeds us crumbs when nobody's looking.

SKWEEK: And she doesn't lay traps to catch us.

SNITCH: No. She leaves that to Grabber!

(General consternation. SNITCH has said a Bad Word.)

ALL MICE: Shhh! Ahhh! Don't say that name!

MAIN MOUSE: It's bad luck to say the Cat's name, you silly little rodent.

SNITCH: Sorry.

MAIN MOUSE: Anyway, she always tells him off afterwards. And gives us a proper funeral with a matchbox and everything. She's nice to mice, is Cinderella. We shouldn't get her into trouble.

SKWEEK: But she's a human. We're mice. You've got to get your priorities right. Our lives are committed to the Glorious Quest for Cheese. Right, gang?

ALL MICE: Right! Cheese! Cheese! Cheese! Chee...

MAIN MOUSE: SHHHHHHH! I think I hear something...

(A rumbling noise, off stage, coming closer.)

MAIN MOUSE: It's Grabber! Run for your lives!

(They scatter and exit in terror.)

Act 1, Scene 1 – Poor Cinderella

The Kitchen. GRABBER leaps on stage, with a bloodcurdling howl.

GRABBER: MIAAAAAOOOOOOW! Mice! I hate 'em. Spit, spit, spit.
Where have they gone? I'll get 'em! I'll pulverise 'em!
I'll make minced mouse meat out of 'em!
MIAAAAOOOOOOOW!

(Enter CINDERELLA.)

CINDERELLA: You'll do nothing of the sort, Grabber!
Get away from that mousehole this instant!
What have I told you about bullying the mice?

GRABBER: I like bullying mice! I like backing 'em into corners and
pulling their silly little whiskers!

CINDERELLA: How <u>could</u> you? Poor little things. You should love them.

GRABBER: I do. All laid out on a plate, with their little tails
coiled round. MIAAAOOOOOW.

CINDERELLA: Well, you should be ashamed of yourself. It's not as though
you don't get enough to eat. You're a very bad cat.

GRABBER: *(sulky)* Miaw-huh.

CINDERELLA: And there's no need to go sulking either.
Now, out you go while I get the floor swept.
If Semolina and Ravioli wake up and breakfast isn't ready,
my life won't be worth living. Go on.

(GRABBER stalks out. CINDERELLA begins to sweep. Enter BUTTONS, carrying a tray and three large envelopes.)

BUTTONS: Morning, Cinderella. Housework again?

CINDERELLA: I'm afraid so, Buttons. That's all I ever seem to do these days.

BUTTONS: You should complain to the Baron.

CINDERELLA: What's the point? Semolina and Ravioli have got him just where they want him. If he tries to take my side, they just stop his pocket money.

BUTTONS: Good. That'll teach him not to marry for money.

CINDERELLA: Poor Daddy. I think he wishes he hadn't.
But it's too late now. It's too late for all of us.
Sometimes I think nothing good will ever happen again.

BUTTONS: Nonsense. In fact, I've got something here that'll cheer you up.

(He hands her an envelope.)

CINDERELLA: What's this?

BUTTONS: It's your invitation. To the ball.

CINDERELLA: What ball?

BUTTONS: Haven't you heard? The Prince is holding a great ball up at the palace. The King says he has to choose a wife. Everyone's invited.

CINDERELLA: What, me as well?

BUTTONS: Of course. There's your name, look.

CINDERELLA: Oh, Buttons. I can't believe it! Just think - an invitation to a real palace ball! It's the sort of thing that only happens in fairy tales.

BUTTONS: You see? I knew that'd cheer you up.

(Off stage, SEMOLINA and RAVIOLI shout for CINDERELLA.)

SISTERS: Cin-der-ella!

CINDERELLA: Oh no! They want their breakfast and I haven't even got the fire laid - and I don't think there's a stick of firewood left.

BUTTONS: Don't worry. You pop out and get some. I'll take their invitations up. That'll keep them quiet for a bit.

CINDERELLA: Oh, thanks, Buttons. You're a good mate.

(She puts the invitation in her pocket, takes her shawl and exits.)

BUTTONS: Good mate, eh? Oh well - I suppose it's better than nothing...

(Sighing, he exits.)

Act 1, Scene 2 – Rotten Relations

The Bedroom. SEMOLINA and RAVIOLI, the Hardup sisters, are sitting up in bed in their nightgowns. Their hair is in curlers. They give huge yawns.

SEMOLINA: How did you sleep last night, Ravioli dear?

RAVIOLI: How d'you think? With my eyes closed. That's when you weren't snoring, Semolina.

SEMOLINA: Do you have to wake up grumpy every morning?

RAVIOLI: I don't. Snow White wakes up Grumpy every morning. Let's look at the menu and get Cinderella to bring us up some breakfast in bed.

SEMOLINA: Ooh yes!

(They take two large menus from under the bedclothes and study them.)

RAVIOLI: Now then. What shall we have?

BREAKFAST SERVED IN BED
(RAVIOLI and SEMOLINA sing to the tune of Old McDonald Had A Farm.)

1. What's the most enormous treat?
    Breakfast served in bed!
    Smearing butter on the sheet,
    Never on your bread.

With a crumpet here and a crumpet there,
Here a crumb, there a crumb, everywhere a toast crumb,
What will make our lives complete?
Breakfast served in bed!

2. What's the most enormous thrill?
    Breakfast served in bed!
    Starting with a big mixed grill
    Served with chocolate spread.

    With a sausage here and a sausage there,
    Here a chip, there a chip, everywhere a burnt chip,
    Crumpet here and a crumpet there,
    Here a crumb, there a crumb, everywhere a toast crumb,
    What's the most enormous thrill?
    Breakfast served in bed!

3. What's the treat we like the most?
    Breakfast served in bed,
    Trying to eat baked beans on toast
    (With a) pillow on your head!

    With a biscuit here and a biscuit there,
    Here a bit, there a bit, everywhere a bis-cuit,
    Sausage here and a sausage there,
    Here a chip, there a chip, everywhere a burnt chip,
    Crumpet here and a crumpet there,
    Here a crumb, there a crumb, everywhere a toast crumb,
    What's the treat we like the most?
    Breakfast Served In Bed!

SEMOLINA: Stir fried crumpets for starters, I think. Got to be healthy.

RAVIOLI: And fish cakes. With jam.

SEMOLINA: And soup on toast. And pork pie with custard and
               roly poly pudding with a marmite sauce, I fancy.

RAVIOLI: And a dreamy creamy, squelchy welchy piece of chocky
               cake with lots of yummy mashed potato. And chips.

SEMOLINA: Right, I think that's everything. Let's ring for Cinderella.

RAVIOLI: No. Let's scream.

(They bellow.)

SISTERS: Cinderella!

RAVIOLI: Oh, and we mustn't forget to order eggs.
Eggs get you cracking in the morning.

SEMOLINA: But prunes get you going.

RAVIOLI: True. But you can't beat eggs.

SEMOLINA: You're so ignorant, Ravioli. Certainly you can beat eggs.
You can whip them too. All that corporal punishment,
sooner or later they'll crack.

RAVIOLI: I'm not so sure. Hard boiled characters, some of them...

(A knock at the door.)

SEMOLINA: Oh, goody. That'll be Cinderella come to take our order.
And about time too.

SISTERS: Enter!

(Enter BUTTONS, with the invitations on a tray.)

BUTTONS: Morning, ladies.

SEMOLINA: Oh. It's just the houseboy.

RAVIOLI: Boring!

SEMOLINA: What do you want, houseboy?

BUTTONS: I've brought you your post.

RAVIOLI: Fan mail, I suppose. More admiring letters from the Big Bad Wolf and Captain Hook.
Pass 'em over, Buttons - and look zippy!

(They scream with laughter. BUTTONS gives them the invitations.)

SEMOLINA: My my! What have we here?

RAVIOLI: Looks like invitations!

(They tear open the envelopes.)

SEMOLINA: Oh my! It's to the Prince's ball! At last! At last! My chance to become a princess!

RAVIOLI: What d'you mean, your chance? If the Prince chooses anyone for his wife, it's sure to be me. Especially when he sees my exotic dancing style.

(Leaps out of bed and demonstrates.)

SEMOLINA: That's rubbish, that is. You've got two left feet.

RAVIOLI: So? Now all I have to do is find a partner with two right ones. Dancers run in our family.
What do you think, Buttons?

BUTTONS: I think it's a great pity they don't dance.

(Screaming, they chase him off with the tray.)

Act 1, Scene 3 – Chance Meetings

The Wood. There is a tree to hide behind and a stump to sit on. We hear the sound of a hunting horn. GRABBER runs across the stage and off.

GRABBER: meeeaaaAAAAAAWWWWWOOOOOOOOOoooooo........

(Enter GARY in hot pursuit, waving a sword.)

GARY: Where'd it go? Where's it gone? Don't you worry, sir,
I'll get it! Come out, you hairy monster!

(Enter PRINCE CHARMING. He watches GARY crashing about for a moment, then gives a sigh.)

PRINCE: Do give it a rest, Gary, will you?

GARY: But I had it cornered, sir. I was that close,
I could see its great, mad, rolling yellow eyes.
I had it cowering at sword point!

PRINCE: So what happened?

GARY: It scratched me on the arm an' ran off. There, look.

PRINCE: Where?

GARY: There. A great gouge. Sabre tooth tiger, I reckon.

PRINCE: Sabre toothed tigers don't wear jolly little red collars
with bells on, Gary. Besides, they're extinct.

GARY: What's that, then, sir?

PRINCE: Gone. Not around any more.

GARY: Well, there you are, then. That proves it.
This one's not around any more.

PRINCE: It was a harmless little kitty cat. Somebody's pet,
probably. For goodness' sake, put your sword away.
Relax. Have a lettuce sandwich.

(He takes out a sandwich.)

GARY: Can't do that, sir. More than my job's worth. A royal
bodyguard's got to be ready at all times. Anyway, I thought
we were going hunting. I've been looking forward to it.
I'm a good hunter, I am.

PRINCE: Really? Have you ever hunted bear?

GARY: Well, no. But I've gone fishing in my shorts.

PRINCE: Well, I don't approve of it. I'm a vegetarian.

GARY: So why did we come to the woods?

PRINCE: To get away from the palace and get a bit of peace and quiet. All this fuss about the ball - it gets on my nerves. I don't even want to get married. Not unless I meet someone I like. Fat chance of that.

GARY: Oh, I wouldn't say that, sir. Lot of invitations gone out. Lots of suitable young ladies coming, sir.

PRINCE: Yes. And they're all rich and snobby and I don't like any of them...

GARY: Sssssh! Something's coming. Probably the tiger coming back. Get behind me, sir, I'll defend you.

(He runs behind the tree.)

PRINCE: Don't be silly, Gary. Here, kitty-kitty...

GARY: Sir! Please! I must insist you get behind this tree. It's for your own safety. Besides, it makes me look bad.

PRINCE: Oh, this is ridiculous...

(Reluctantly he allows himself to be tugged behind the tree. Enter CINDERELLA, being pulled by GRABBER.)

CINDERELLA: All right, then, so where is this great big wild-eyed cat-hater with the giant sword?

GRABBER: Miaow! Well, he was here a minute ago. Out to get me for sure. Nearly did, too.

CINDERELLA: Well, I don't see him now. And now you know what it's like to be chased, maybe you'll leave the mice alone.

GRABBER: Huh. That's the trouble with you, Cinderella. You always take the side of the underdog. Miaow.

CINDERELLA: Undermouse, actually.

GRABBER: Pthhhhht! I'm going back to tell on you.

CINDERELLA: Oh, Grabber, please don't do that. I'm in enough trouble as it is... Grabber? (GRABBER stalks off.) Oh dear. That's all I need. Why doesn't anything ever go right?

(Wearily, she begins to gather firewood. The lights dim. A low rumble of thunder.)

CINDERELLA: My, it's getting very dark. I hope there won't be a storm.

(A loud clap of thunder. Enter an OLD WOMAN in a long cloak.)

OLD WOMAN: Good morning, my dear.

CINDERELLA: Goodness! You startled me.

OLD WOMAN: Nothing to be afraid of, deary. I won't harm you. I'm just out gathering a few sticks for the fire. To warm my old bones in this cold weather.

CINDERELLA: (sympathetically) Back trouble, is it? Father gets that. You should try an apple a day. That keeps the doctor away.

OLD WOMAN: I prefer a clove of garlic. That keeps everyone away. Ooh me back, me back.

(Wearily, she sits on the stump.)

CINDERELLA: You shouldn't be out collecting sticks in your state of health. If I made the laws around here, I'd make fuel freely available for the over sixties.

PRINCE: (calls out) Jolly good idea... mff mff...

(GARY claps his hand over the PRINCE's mouth.)

CINDERELLA: *(startled)* What was that?

OLD WOMAN: Just a bird, I think.

PRINCE: Er... tweet tweet?

OLD WOMAN: Just a bird. Ah well. Better be getting on...

(She rises.)

CINDERELLA: Look, take my firewood. I can get some more.

OLD WOMAN: Really? Well, it's very sweet of you, deary.
You're a kind lass. Maybe somebody will do you a good turn
one of these days, Cinderella.

(She hobbles off.)

CINDERELLA: I doubt it, somehow. I wonder how she knew my name?
Ah, well...

(Sighing, CINDERELLA exits. PRINCE CHARMING and GARY come out from hiding.)

PRINCE: *(excitedly)* Did you see that, Gary? A genuine act
of kindness. You don't see that much nowadays.
And that idea about free fuel was brilliant. Nice name, too.
Cinderella. Sort of...

GARY: Long?

PRINCE: That's it. What a charming girl.

GARY: I thought <u>you</u> were Charming.

PRINCE: I am. But she's even more so.

GARY: But she's poor.

PRINCE: So?

GARY:	She was all ragged. She didn't even have shoes on.
PRINCE:	I don't care! I'm going after her. There are things I want to ask her.
GARY:	Like what?
PRINCE:	Like - does she play polo? That'll do for a start. Or perhaps she might like a sandwich.
GARY:	Forget it, sir. She's just a simple peasant girl. You're Prince Charming. You'd frighten the life out of her, with your royal sandwiches. She'd get all tongue tied.
PRINCE:	(sadly) Do you really think so? They are lettuce...
GARY:	Come on, sir. Let's go back to the palace. I'll get the cook to do you a nice nut roast...

(He coaxes a reluctant PRINCE off stage.)

Act 1, Scene 4 – Great News!

The Kitchen. BUTTONS is polishing shoes. Enter the SISTERS with GRABBER.

SEMOLINA:	Where's Cinderella, Buttons? We want a word with her.
RAVIOLI:	She didn't bring us breakfast in bed.
SEMOLINA:	And the fire's not lit.
RAVIOLI:	And she's been mean to Grabber again, hasn't she darling? Taking the side of the mice. You've got mouse withdrawal symptoms, haven't you, poor little puddy tat?

(GRABBER rubs against her, purring. Enter CINDERELLA.)

SEMOLINA:	Ah! There you are!
RAVIOLI:	You didn't bring breakfast!

SEMOLINA: And Grabber says you've been picking on him.

CINDERELLA: Oh, Grabber, you fibber. I did nothing of the sort...

SEMOLINA: You see? She's doing it again. Come to mummy, diddums.

RAVIOLI: Where've you been, anyway? And what's that you've got in your pocket?

SEMOLINA: Hand it over.

CINDERELLA: No. It's mine. It's my invitation.

SEMOLINA: *(snapping her fingers)* Come on. Give.

BUTTONS: Don't do it, Cinderella...

RAVIOLI: Look! Cinderella! What's that behind you?

(CINDERELLA looks. SEMOLINA snatches the invitation.)

SEMOLINA: She's right. It's an invitation to the ball.

(RAVIOLI snatches it, examines it and tears it up.)

RAVIOLI: *(smugly)* <u>Was</u> an invitation, you mean.

(They shriek with laughter.)

CINDERELLA: Ravioli, that was <u>mean!</u> That's the meanest thing you've ever done...

(Enter BARON HARDUP. He is a tottery old gentleman with a stick and an ear trumpet.)

BARON: Now, now, girls - what's all this?

(The SISTERS run to him and sob on his shoulder.)

SEMOLINA: Oh, Daddy. Cinderella's attacking us. Just because we tore up her silly old invitation to the ball.

RAVIOLI:	She can't go anyway, can she, Daddy? Somebody's got to stay behind and give Grabber his supper.
SEMOLINA:	And she hasn't got a dress.
CINDERELLA:	You'll buy me a dress, won't you, Father?
BARON:	*(doubtfully)* Well, I... er...
SEMOLINA:	Oh no he won't. We control the purse strings around here, don't we, Ravioli?
RAVIOLI:	We certainly do. Tell her, Daddy.
BARON:	It's true, Cinderella. There's nothing I can do about it. I don't have a bean of my own. Ah me, what it is to be such a weak character. And I don't get to say much either.
SEMOLINA:	Off you go, Daddy.
BARON:	You see?

(He exits sadly.)

RAVIOLI:	Come on, Semolina. Let's go and try on our dresses for the ball.

(They exit. CINDERELLA picks up the pieces of torn invitation and tries to fit them together. She gives up, sits down and bursts into tears. BUTTONS tries to comfort her.)

BUTTONS:	Oh, come on, Cinders. Don't cry. Look, what about a nice cup of tea? I'll make it just how you like it.
CINDERELLA:	No thanks, Buttons. You're very kind - but if you don't mind, I think I'd like to be left alone for a while.

(BUTTONS exits. CINDERELLA continues to weep. Lights dim. After a pause, the MICE creep in and watch CINDERELLA.)

SKWEEK:	Well, that was a bit of a downer.

TIPTOE: Terrible. Anyone got a tissue?

LONGTAIL: I had one, but I ate it.

WETNOSE: I'm so depressed I don't even feel like cheese.

SNITCH: Can't we do something about it?

SKWEEK: Like what? I mean, we're mice. We're limited.

TIPTOE: Any ideas, Main Mouse?

MAIN MOUSE: *(sighing)* I dunno. It's the size, isn't it? I keep thinking it's a pity we aren't horses.

WETNOSE: Horses? What's he talking about, horses?

MAIN MOUSE: It's silly, I know. But I keep thinking how good it would be if we could grow in size and hitch ourselves up to a carriage and take her out somewhere nice...

(The MICE fall about laughing.)

SKWEEK: Horses! What a stupid idea! Sometimes I wonder about you, Main Mouse...

MAIN MOUSE: All right, all right, it was just a thought. Just because I'm a mouse. There's no need to take the Micky.

LONGTAIL: You know what? I don't want to hang around here any more. It's too depressing. Let's go back to the hole and talk about cheese.

SNITCH: *(unenthusiastically)* Oh yeah. Let's.

(All exit, the MICE chanting a despondent dirge.)

ALL MICE: Cheese! Cheese! Cheese! Cheese...

INTERVAL

Act 2, Scene 1 – The Transformation

The Kitchen. The lights come up. CINDERELLA looks up as BUTTONS comes in.

BUTTONS: They're coming! If this doesn't make you laugh,
Cinderella, nothing will!

(Enter SEMOLINA and RAVIOLI, followed by GRABBER. The SISTERS are dressed to kill. CINDERELLA stifles a giggle.)

SEMOLINA: Here we are then, all dressed up with somewhere to go. *(twirling)* So what do you think of the get-up?

(She takes an enormous comb from her bag and fiddles with her hair. RAVIOLI takes out a tub of powder and liberally powders her nose.)

BUTTONS: Achoo! Indescribable. What's that lovely perfume you're wearing? Don't tell me! *(sniffs)* Compost Nights, yes?

SEMOLINA: Don't be cheeky, houseboy. Go and get the carriage ready. And tell Daddy we're ready to leave.

(BUTTONS exits.)

RAVIOLI: And you can get this kitchen cleared up while we're gone, Cinderella. I don't know. The trouble with servants these days. Look, there's bits of paper all over the floor.

CINDERELLA: Yes, and whose fault is that?

SEMOLINA: Ooh, temper temper. She's jealous, look, Ravioli.
She wishes she could go to the ball.

RAVIOLI: She could, if it was fancy dress.
She could go as a scarecrow. On a dustcart.

CINDERELLA: You're horrible. You're the horriblest sisters in the world.

RAVIOLI: We know.

SEMOLINA: We like it. It's fun. Look, Ravioli, she's crying.

CINDERELLA: Oh no I'm not.

SISTERS: Oh yes you are.

RAVIOLI: We'd stay and jeer at you some more, Cinderella, but we just don't have the time, do we, Semo?

SEMOLINA: Don't forget to give Grabber his plate of lobster. On the dot, mind.

GRABBER: Got that? On the dot.

SEMOLINA: And we shan't want breakfast. We'll be sleeping in late in the morning, after dancing the night away. Come on, Ravioli - it's party time!

(Triumphantly, they exit, followed by GRABBER. CINDERELLA is left alone.)

CINDERELLA: Well, that's it, then. Everybody's off to the ball but me.

(She sighs. The lights dim.)

THEY'VE ALL GONE OUT DANCING BUT ME
(CINDERELLA sings to the tune of My Bonny Lies Over The Ocean.)

I'm left all alone in the kitchen,
I'm feeling as sad as can be,
It seems the whole world has gone dancing,
They've all gone out dancing but me.

Dancing, dancing,
They've all gone out dancing but me, but me,
Dancing, dancing,
They've all gone out dancing but me.

The lights will be bright at the palace,
I see them so clear in my mind,
Oh, how could they all go out dancing
And leave Cinderella behind?

Dancing, dancing,
They've all gone out dancing but me, but me,
Dancing, dancing,
They've all gone out dancing but me.

(There is a rumble of thunder, followed by a knock at the door.)

CINDERELLA: Now, who can that be, I wonder?

(OLD WOMAN enters.)

CINDERELLA: Why, it's you again!

OLD WOMAN: Yes, my dear. Prepare yourself for a wonderful surprise. I'm about to reveal my true self. Just waiting for the thunderclap.

(A thunderclap. She throws off her cloak and reveals herself as the FAIRY GODMOTHER in a seriously glittering dress. She brandishes a wand.)

GODMOTHER: Yes, Cinderella - I am none other than your Fairy Godmother, come to grant you a wish. *(She winces and holds her back.)* Ouch.

CINDERELLA: How's your poor back?

GODMOTHER: Terrible. But I'm a fairy. I have to rise above such things. Now let's not talk about me. Let's talk about your wish. I can't wait to get to the bit where I say, "You shall go to the ball!"

CINDERELLA: But how do you know that's what I want?

GODMOTHER: Just a shrewd guess. I'm right, aren't I?

CINDERELLA: Well, yes, but...

GODMOTHER: Then let's get on with it. Cinderella, you shall go to the ball!

(There is a pause.)

CINDERELLA: Er... shouldn't something happen?

GODMOTHER: Oh, it's not as simple as that. You have to help a bit.
        Pop outside and bring me a pumpkin from the garden.
        Hurry up, we haven't got all night.

CINDERELLA   A <u>pumpkin</u>?

(Bewildered, she shrugs, takes her shawl and exits.)

GODMOTHER: This is where I would normally do a dance.
        But on account of my back, I shall sing a song instead.

(Lights dim further.)

GOTTA GET YOURSELF A FAIRY
(The FAIRY GODMOTHER sings to the tune of In An English Country Garden.)

What do you need when things are going wrong
And the path of life gets hairy?
I'll tell you all in a jolly little song –
Gotta get yourself a fairy.

Flitting here and flitting there,
Pretty spangles in her hair,
Nice pair of wings
And an hour to spare,
With a wave of her wand
She can banish your despair,
Gotta get yourself a fairy.

What do you need when nothing's going well
And you're feeling kind of tearful?
She'll come along with a simple little spell
And she'll leave you feeling cheerful.

Flitting here and flitting there,
Pretty spangles in her hair,
Nice pair of wings
And an hour to spare,
With a wave of her wand
She can banish your despair
And she'll leave you feeling cheerful.

(Enter "CINDERELLA." She gives the pumpkin to the FAIRY. Note: this is a substitute CINDERELLA. She is a different actress wearing CINDERELLA's ragged dress and shawl. The real CINDERELLA is changing into her ballgown off stage.)

GODMOTHER: Perfect. Now all we need are some mice.

(Enter MICE at a run.)

MAIN MOUSE: Did you say <u>mice</u>?
Well, don't look twice.

SKWEEK: We're yours to command
For a very small price

TIPTOE: We've skulked too long
In our wee small hole

LONGTAIL: And now we are ready
For a starring role!

WETNOSE: There's not a lot
That we won't do...

SNITCH: For a hunk of cheese
And a crumb or two.

ALL MICE: If you need some mice
To help the plot...
Well, look no further,
Mice you've got!

GODMOTHER: Good gracious! Well, we're certainly well off for volunteers.
Too many, in fact. I'll take you - and you - and you -

(She selects MAIN MOUSE, LONGTAIL, TIPTOE, SKWEEK, WETNOSE and SNITCH from the total number of MICE.)

GODMOTHER: Sorry, the rest of you. Don't ring us, we'll ring you.

REJECTED MICE: Typical. Just because we don't squeak so loud...

(The rejected MICE exit, moaning.)

GODMOTHER: Right. Mice, take this pumpkin into the garden. Count to ten and stand well back. We don't want any accidents. You have to be careful with magic.

(Exit the chosen MICE with the pumpkin. Thunder rumbles. The lights dim even further.)

GODMOTHER: Now at last this tale so tragic
Gets a helping hand from magic.
Now's the time for revelation
Miracles and transformation.
Cinderella, dry your eyes
Prepare yourself for a surprise.
A fairy coach, a fancy dress
At last you are a real princess.

(The FAIRY GODMOTHER waves her wand. The lights come up. Ceiling lights can be switched off and on again here. A fanfare is heard off stage. The coach comes on stage, masking the substitute CINDERELLA, who exits, to be replaced by the real CINDERELLA. The coach is pulled by MAIN MOUSE, SKWEEK, LONGTAIL and WETNOSE. They are now horses. TIPTOE and SNITCH are now footmen. The real CINDERELLA steps out from behind the coach.)

CINDERELLA: Oh, Godmother! It's beautiful. I love it!

GODMOTHER: One of my successes, I think. Now off you go and enjoy yourself. But the magic only lasts until midnight, mind, so make sure you leave before then.

CINDERELLA: I will. Goodbye. And thank you!

GODMOTHER: Goodbye, Cinderella. And don't forget - make sure you leave before the last stroke of twelve.

(CINDERELLA climbs into the coach. All exit.)

Act 2, Scene 2 – Having A Ball!

The Palace Ballroom. Music plays in the background. COURTIERS and GUESTS talk in groups. PRINCE CHARMING chats despondently to GARY.

PRINCE: You see? What did I tell you? I knew it wouldn't be my sort of do.

GARY: Cheer up, sir. Here. Have a peanut.

PRINCE: No thanks. I'm not hungry. It's like being at a cattle market. It's disgusting. Particularly to a vegetarian.

GARY: They haven't all arrived yet. Maybe the best is yet to come.

(The FOOTMAN enters. He makes his announcement to a fanfare.)

FOOTMAN: *(announcing)* The Baron Hardup and his two lovely daughters, Lady Semolina and Lady Ravioli!

(Enter the BARON, with SEMOLINA and RAVIOLI.)

GARY: On the other hand, perhaps not.

SEMOLINA: Isn't it lovely, Ravioli? Too, too tasteful.

RAVIOLI: There's the Prince, look. Coo-ee! Prince Charming! Bags I the first dance!

SEMOLINA: Me, you mean!

(They push each other, glaring, then begin to advance.)

PRINCE: Help! They're coming over!

(Another fanfare stops them in their tracks.)

FOOTMAN: The Princess Crystal from the Isle of Mistique!

(Enter CINDERELLA.)

PRINCE: Good heavens! She's new.

GARY: Nice dress.

PRINCE: There's something about her... She reminds me of someone...

GARY: Well, don't hang about, sir. Ask her to dance.

PRINCE: I will. I jolly well will. Er - excuse me, Your Highness. May I have the pleasure?

CINDERELLA: Why, of course.

(CINDERELLA and the PRINCE, the GUESTS and COURTIERS dance.)

SEMOLINA: Well! What a nerve!

RAVIOLI: Taking him over like that.

SEMOLINA: We ought to complain.

RAVIOLI: We will.

SISTERS: Daddy!

(They flounce over to complain to BARON HARDUP, who pats them ineffectually. The dance ends.)

PRINCE: I'm sure I know you from somewhere.

CINDERELLA: I don't think so.

PRINCE: I do, you know. For some reason, a certain phrase keeps coming into my mind. You're not over sixty, by any chance?

CINDERELLA: (with a laugh) Charming!

PRINCE: Yes, that's me, I'm afraid. I'd sooner have been called Butch, but it's too late now. But enough of me. I want to hear all about you. You're not a vegetarian, by any chance?

CINDERELLA: As a matter of fact, I am.

PRINCE: You are? Oh, splendid, splendid. They grow a lot of vegetables, then, do they? On Mistique?

CINDERELLA: Oh - er - yes. Lots. You can't move for carrots sometimes.

PRINCE: <u>Really</u>? Fascinating. Supposed to be good for the eyes, carrots. The trouble is, I nearly go blind when I stick them in.

(Much to his relief, CINDERELLA laughs at his joke. GARY taps his shoulder.)

GARY: Excuse me, sir...

PRINCE: Go away, Gary. Can't you see I'm making amusing conversation? Tell me, Princess Crystal, do you have an opinion about lettuces? Personally, I don't think you can beat a nice crisp lettuce sandwich, do you?

CINDERELLA: Oh, absolutely not.

PRINCE: I say! We really do have a lot in common, don't we?

GARY: Sir, I don't want to interrupt, but isn't it time you made - you know. The Announcement. The ladies are getting impatient.

PRINCE: Yes, yes, all in good time, Gary. I'm having an in-depth discussion here! So tell me, Crystal, where exactly <u>is</u> the Isle of Mistique? If it's not far, I thought I might row over one Saturday, bring a picnic lunch or something? What d'you think?

(Suddenly, the lights dim. The clock begins to strike midnight. The action freezes. We hear the GODMOTHER's voice.)

GODMOTHER: The midnight hour has come at last!
The magic spell is weakening fast.
Make haste! You're running out of time.
You have to beat that final chime.

CINDERELLA:	Oh no! Is that the time? I must go...

(CINDERELLA exits, leaving her shoe.)

PRINCE:	Come back! At least give me a contact address! Or a fax number!
GARY:	Too late, sir. She's gone. <u>But she left this!</u>

(He picks up the shoe and presents it with a flourish.)

PRINCE:	(clasping it ecstatically) A shoe! A shoe!
GARY:	Nasty cold you've got there.
PRINCE:	Right, that's it. I've made up my mind. Whoever's foot fits this shoe shall be my bride! And that's an official proclamation. I shall be coming around tomorrow with this on a cushion. So be ready and wash your feet!
GARY:	That's a bit risky, sir, isn't it? I mean, it might fit anybody. It might fit me! Hey! I could be a princess!
PRINCE:	Don't be ridiculous. You only have to look at it to know this shoe is special. I can tell. Have faith, Gary. We'll find her yet!

(All exit.)

Act 2, Scene 3 – The Shoe Fits

The Kitchen. The following day. The SISTERS are waiting to try on the shoe. They wiggle their toes expectantly through the holes in their stockings. GRABBER watches.

SEMOLINA:	Ooh, I can't wait, Ravioli. Now's my big chance. If you're very good, I might let you be my bridesmaid.
RAVIOLI:	Don't count on it, pasty feet. What size are you again?
SEMOLINA:	Eight. Double W fitting.

RAVIOLI: Well, there you are then. Much too big. I'm a size four.

SEMOLINA: Oh no you're not.

RAVIOLI: Oh yes I am. It's just that I always wear size seven because four hurts my toes.

(Enter BUTTONS. He sees them and attempts to leave.)

RAVIOLI: Come back here, houseboy. Now, be honest. We want you to examine our feet and tell us whose are the biggest.

BUTTONS: That's a sole searching question.

(Holding his nose, he advances and inspects their feet.)

BUTTONS: You've got odd socks on.

RAVIOLI: I know. The funny thing is, I've got another pair just like it.

(A knock at the door.)

SEMOLINA: That's him! It's his Royal Highness! Answer the door, then, houseboy. And be quick about it, or it's the buttonhook for you.

(BUTTONS opens the door. Enter PRINCE and GARY with the shoe on a cushion.)

RAVIOLI: Oh my! I feel quite faint!

PRINCE: Morning, ladies.

SEMOLINA: He spoke, he spoke!

PRINCE: Right, let's make this snappy, shall we? Let's have the shoe, Gary. Now, who's first?

SISTERS: Me!

PRINCE: Alphabetical order. Ravioli first.

RAVIOLI: Hah!

(She snatches it and tries it on without success.)

PRINCE: Sorry. Not a chance. Next?

SEMOLINA: My turn! Me!

(She tries on the shoe. She hobbles round with it on her toe.)

SEMOLINA: There. Perfect.

PRINCE: Nonsense, it's miles too small.

(He picks it up and sets it on the cushion.)

PRINCE: So it's just you two here, is it? Nobody else?

RAVIOLI: *(sulkily)* Just us. That's right. Isn't it, Semo?

SEMOLINA: Oh dear me yes, Ravi. Nobody else.

BUTTONS: Oh yes there is.

SISTERS: Shut up, houseboy!

BUTTONS: I won't shut up. *(calls)* Cinderella! Come in here a moment! You're wanted!

SISTERS: Oh no she isn't.

BUTTONS: Oh yes she is!

SISTERS: Oh no she isn't!

BUTTONS: *(conducting audience)* <u>Oh yes she is!</u>

(CINDERELLA enters hesitantly.)

CINDERELLA: Did someone call? *(sees PRINCE)* Oh - it's you!

PRINCE: It's her! The girl in the woods! Free fuel for the
                     over sixties – right?

BUTTONS: Sit down, Cinderella. Try on the shoe.

(CINDERELLA tries on the shoe. A drum roll. The action freezes. Enter MICE.)

MAIN MOUSE: This is the moment when wrongs get righted.

LONGTAIL: When kings get crowned.

TIPTOE: When knights get knighted.

WETNOSE: When justice triumphs.

SKWEEK: When cheese gets eaten...

ALL MICE: And all the baddies
                     Know they're beaten.

MAIN MOUSE: And it's only right that us mice are here to witness it.
                     After all our hard work filling in the background.

SKWEEK: And pulling that coach. That was no picnic.

ALL MICE: Our story ends in the nicest way.
                     The slipper fits! Hip hip, hooray!

(Everybody cheers.)

MAIN MOUSE: Now let's go home and take our ease
                     And celebrate with lots of...

ALL MICE: CHEEEEEESE!

Act 2, Scene 4 – Happy Ever After

The Kitchen. The curtain call takes place at the front of the stage. Enter FOOTMAN.

FOOTMAN: Ladies and Gentlemen - put your hands together for
             BARON HARDUP.

(Enter BARON.)

BARON: Well, thank you very much. I'd just like to say a few words...

FOOTMAN: Move along, if you please.

BARON: You see? Every time.

(The disappointed BARON takes his bow and moves to one side, muttering. The FOOTMAN introduces the following characters, who enter and take their bow:)

GUESTS and COURTIERS

SEMOLINA and RAVIOLI HARDUP

GRABBER THE CAT and BUTTONS

GARY THE GUARD

THE FAIRY GODMOTHER

PRINCE CHARMING and CINDERELLA

FOOTMAN: And a big hand for the MICE!

(The MICE take their bow, along with stage management, scene painters, choir, orchestra, teachers, parents and anyone else involved in the production. Everyone breaks into a rousing reprise of a favourite song.)

THE END

Staging

Area for Performance

You will need to stage *Cinderella* to suit the acting space that you have available. Your school may have its own theatre, with a stage. Or you may be in a position to create your acting area at one end of the school hall, using rostra blocks.

If you do have rostra blocks, you can construct your stage on different levels, to create different areas for each location. The kitchen can be set up in one area, and the wood in another. The wood can become the bedroom, and the kitchen can be turned into the ballroom, by changing the props or scenery.

If you do have a theatre with a fixed stage, and rostra blocks as well, you could use the blocks to build out the stage at the front, creating new areas for different locations, such as the wood, as shown in the diagram below.

But it may be that the only space you have available is the space at the front of the classroom. It is quite possible to perform *Cinderella* in this space, using the minimum of props.

Backdrops

You don't have to have backdrops. One of the actors can carry a sign which says, for example, *The Kitchen at Hardup Hall*. This is an easy way to indicate a location.

If you do decide to make backdrops, you will need to work out how to display them, or hang them, at the back of your stage area. They are quite simple to make. Once you have worked out the size the backdrop should be, you can stick together the right number of large sheets of paper with brown masking tape. Draw an outline of the background scene first, and then paint in the colour.

Scenery and Props

There are eight scenes in *Cinderella* which take place in four different locations: the kitchen, the wood, the bedroom and the palace ballroom. There is also one special prop to make for Act 2, scene 1, which is Cinderella's coach. You can show your audience these scenes with the minimum of props, or you can make more elaborate scenery if you prefer. Here are some ideas:

The Kitchen
Most of the action of the play takes place in the kitchen. The only essential props are a table and a chair to sit on. The table should have a large piece of cheese on it!

The Palace Ballroom
If you are not using a backdrop depicting a ballroom complete with pillars, chandeliers, sweeping steps and so on, some balloons, streamers, and paper chains would indicate the grandeur of the location nicely.

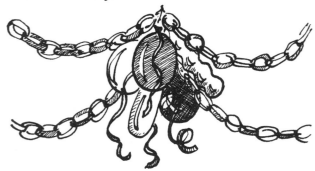

The Bedroom
The stepsisters are in bed throughout most of the scene. The bed can consist quite simply of a large blanket and pillows - raised on rostra blocks if this is possible. Alternatively, you might be able to beg or borrow a camp bed.

The Wood
You will need to make at least one large, freestanding tree. The tree shape can be cut out from strong cardboard and then painted or decorated. You can make a support for the back of the tree like this:

1. Cut out the support from a sheet of strong cardboard and fold along the dotted lines as shown on the diagram below. The length of the support should be the same as the height of your tree. Make your tree a Christmas tree shape.

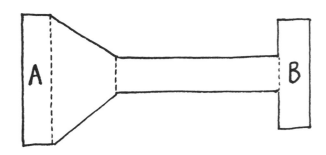

2. The support should be attached to the back of your tree. Fix flap A at the base of the tree. Position flap B slightly higher than halfway up the back of the tree. Adjust flap B before sticking it in place, so that your tree looks like this from the back. Your tree should lean backwards a little.

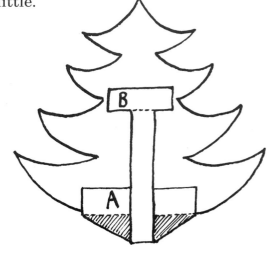

Scenery and Props

Cinderella's Coach

When you read Act 2, scene 1 (the transformation scene) you will notice that the real Cinderella leaves the stage to fetch the Fairy Godmother a pumpkin. A substitute Cinderella, dressed in Cinderella's ragged costume, returns. This will allow the real Cinderella time to change into her ballgown off stage.

Once the substitute Cinderella has given the pumpkin to the Fairy Godmother she should move quietly into the background, and to the side of the stage. The real Cinderella will come on to the stage hidden behind the coach. The coach should come to a halt in front of the substitute Cinderella, so that she can slip off stage discreetly.

The coach can be made from cardboard and a piece of thick material. The coach is carried on and off by the mice.

First, cut out the shape of the roof of the coach from cardboard. Then cut a piece of material to the right width for the body of the coach. Cut out a small square hole for the window. Staple the fabric body of the coach firmly to the cardboard roof. Attach two pieces of dowling to the roof with strong tape, so that the coach can be easily carried by the mice. You may want to staple cardboard strips to the back of the fabric body of the coach to strengthen it. If you would like to make a really elaborate coach for Cinderella, you could staple cardboard wheels to the front.

Props

There are a few other simple props required for each scene. It is a good idea to set up a props table backstage. Each actor can collect their own props from it.

A shawl on Cinderella's chair (Prologue)

A tray and three large invitations (Act 1, scene 1 and Act 1, scene 2)

Two large menus (Act 1, scene 2)

Lettuce sandwiches (Act 1, sc. 3)

A few sticks (Act 1, sc. 3)

Two or three pairs of shoes (Act 1, sc. 4)

Cinderella's invitation (Act 1, sc. 4)

Two large, battered handbags for Ravioli and Semolina (Act 2, sc. 1)

A comb for Semolina (Act 2, sc. 1)

A tub of powder/chalk (Act 2, sc. 1)

A pumpkin (Act 2, sc. 1)

A cushion with Cinderella's shoe on it (Act 2, sc. 3)

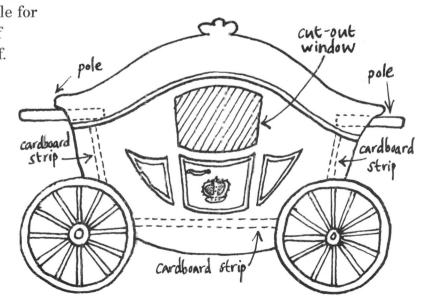

cut-out window

pole

pole

cardboard strip

cardboard strip

cardboard strip

Lighting

If you are able to borrow or hire theatrical lighting, you will be able to follow the lighting instructions within the playscript (Lights Up, Lights Dim) and so on.

You could light your acting area with ordinary ceiling lights. They should be turned off during scene changes.

You might like to turn them off and on again quickly during the transformation scene (Act 2, scene 1) at the moment when the Fairy Godmother is working her spell. They should be on again when the coach arrives on stage.

Casting and Auditions

How Will I Cast the Play?

Diplomatically. I suggest that you hold an initial meeting with all the children who are keen to be involved. You will, of course, be inundated with wildly enthusiastic would-be thespians - but do not panic.

Settle the children down quietly and talk to them about the story of the play and the characters in it (see pages 42-43: The Main Characters). Remind the children that they will need to spend quite a lot of time learning lines and taking directions, especially if they have a large speaking part. Tell them that, although putting on a performance is great fun, it also needs to be taken seriously.

Now you might mention the other desirable alternatives to acting, such as being in the choir or orchestra, or being one of the dancers. Explain the function of the stage management team (see page 44). Point out that every aspect of the production is vitally important.

At this stage many of the children will gravitate in other directions, so announce forthcoming auditions for the choir, orchestra and dancers. You will find that you can include everyone who wants to take an active part in the production.

Casting and Auditions

The Auditions

If you teach drama with children, you will have your own ideas about the auditions. If you feel less certain about this, the following approach may prove helpful:

• Calm the children down. They should concentrate with their eyes shut as you describe a scene from the play; for example, the mice creeping out into the kitchen and pinching some cheese (but keeping an eye open for the cat).

• Ask them to show you the scene. You are the sleeping cat, and they have to sneak up and pinch some cheese from between your feet.

• Make them work in pairs. Give them a task to do together: for example, at your signal, one child must change from a mouse into a footman; the other should register amazement at the transformation.

• Divide them into groups and ask them to improvise the important moment in the transformation scene. At first, the children should act as if they are mice. Then the Fairy Godmother waves her wand, and the mice should change into footmen and horses. Cinderella's rags are transformed. The footmen assist Cinderella into the coach and she is carried off to the ball.

After the group improvisation, you will be able to see which children have the ability to concentrate and can immerse themselves in a role. At this point, you could distribute scripts for a 'read through' the following day.

• Before the read through, divide the children into groups. Let them have a go at several different scenes before making your final decision about the main roles.

Children who are very keen, but not quite ready to handle a large speaking part, could be given a smaller speaking part, or invited to become part of the stage management team.

The Main Characters

Prince Charming
Misunderstood.
Likeable. Sensitive.

The Stepsisters
Mean, sneaky, vain and
horrible, of course - but
hilariously funny.

Baron Hardup
Kind but timid. Afraid his
stepdaughters will stop
his pocket money.

Cinderella
Sweet, kind and good -
but with plenty of spirit.

Gary the Guard
Sweet but dim.
A shocking coward.

Fairy Godmother
Suffers from back trouble.
Has a good sense of humour.

Buttons
Cinderella's best friend.
A cheery, cheeky type.

The Footman
Needs a good, strong voice
and an impressive wig.

Grabber the Cat
Spoilt, with a very vicious streak.

The Mice
These are very rhythmic mice with a
strong common interest in cheese.

The Stage Management Team

The stage management team should consist of at least five children. Theirs is an important role, and they should be involved in rehearsals from the start.

The team could be given specific tasks - they can be involved in as many of these jobs as you think necessary.

Props Table
One of the team should be responsible for seeing that all the personal props are ready on the props table for the actors to collect before the play starts.

Scene Shifters
Two or more children could be put in charge of carrying large props and pieces of scenery on and off, and, if necessary, changing the backdrops. They might also sweep the stage during the interval.

Lighting
If you are using ceiling lights, one member of the team should have a copy of the playscript, marked with their cues to turn them on and off.
(If you are using hired theatrical lighting, an adult will supervise this in any case.)

Sound Effects
One member of the team might be in charge of making the sound effects (see page 48). They should have a playscript, marked with their cues.

Prompter
One child can act as prompter. He or she should be seated off stage with a copy of the playscript, ready to remind the actors of their lines.

Front of House
Two members of the team could be made responsible for arranging the seating and handing out programmes.

Director's Assistant
Your right-hand man or woman, who takes messages, makes lists, reminds you of things and makes sure you've always got a nice cup of tea when you need one.

Rehearsal Schedule

At this point, you will need to draw up a rehearsal schedule. Must rehearsals take place at lunchtime, or can some time be set aside during school hours? How much support can you expect from your head teacher, and the other teachers?

You will need to work out a definite rehearsal plan from the beginning, with times set aside for the final run through, and the dress rehearsal.

Costume

It's probably best to keep the costumes quite simple. Of course, your school may be one of those with a wonderful wardrobe of costumes, built up over the years. More often though, costumes mean lots of enthusiastic work with crepe paper, glue and the staple gun. You will also need to ask parents if their children can bring in some leggings and T-shirts to form the basis of their costume.

Female roles

A costume for any of the female courtiers can be made from a leotard and two skirts. One skirt can be used as the underskirt and one as the overskirt. The overskirt can be bunched up and pinned to the underskirt with large safety pins covered with bows. The leotard top could be suitably decorated.

Fairy Godmother

The Fairy Godmother needs a cloak with a hood which could be made from a large piece of old material. An old ballet tutu would be perfect for her dress, if possible. Don't forget her magic wand!

Cinderella

Cinderella needs to have two costumes - a ragged costume and a smart ballgown. There may be a parent who can lend an ex-bridesmaid's dress for this purpose, or you can make her dress as shown on the left. She also needs smart shoes. Ballet slippers would be very suitable.

Cinderella (and the substitute) require a ragged costume each.

1. Make a simple tunic by joining together two rectangles of material across the shoulder seams.

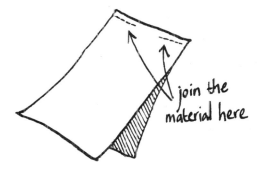

join the material here

2. To give her costume a ragged effect, sew patches on to the tunic, and cut out zig-zag shapes from the bottom hem.

patches →

zig-zag shapes

3. A short apron completes her costume.

apron

Costume

Male roles

A costume for Prince Charming or any of the courtiers, can easily be made from leggings and a shirt, with the leggings tucked into wellington boots and paper cuffs attached to the shirt cuffs, or tucked around the top of the wellington boots. Paper cuffs can be made from thin card and lace paper doilies.

Buttons

Buttons only needs a tracksuit top and leggings and of course, large, shiny buttons. These buttons can be made from ordinary badges covered with silver foil, and then pinned on to the costume.

Prince Charming

He can wear leggings rolled up at the knee, decorated with paper rosettes. A pair of ordinary black shoes can be dressed up with large ribbon bows.

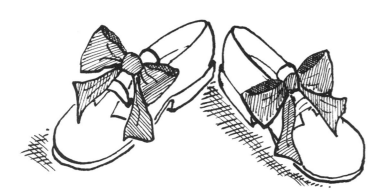

Gary the Guard

Gary needs a sword (made from card and covered in silver foil). His boots and sweatshirt top could be decorated with regimental stripes cut from adhesive-backed plastic.

The Footman

He requires a wig. This can be made from a double page of a large newspaper. Fold the newspaper into eight layers and make cuts into it as shown:

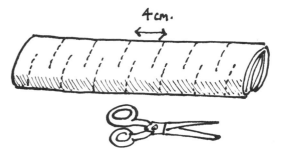

After that, unwrap the wig very carefully. Once the wig has been placed on the child's head, you should attach two lengths of wool to each side of the wig and tie them together under the chin. This will keep the wig from slipping. The paper wig is very easy and quick to make, but it will tear eventually. It would be a good idea to make some spares!

Baron Hardup

If a long coat can be begged or borrowed, this would suit the Baron. He also requires a stick and an ear trumpet. The trumpet could be made from a plastic funnel, covered with papier-maché, and sprayed silver.

Costume

Unisex Roles

Ravioli and Semolina

If these parts are played by boys, they will, of course, wear dresses, in the best pantomime tradition. In the bedroom scene, both Ugly Sisters should wear frilly nighties and have paper curlers in their hair.

Their costumes for the ball should be as outrageous as possible: dresses and Dr Martens, lots of scarves, topped with extravagant hats. They should wear socks and tights with lots of holes in. Ravioli should have odd socks on.

The Horses

Adapt the template shown on the right to make the horse masks. Again, the actors might like to make and decorate their own masks.

Horse tails can be made quite easily by using an assortment of 50cm lengths of string, wool, raffia and strips of paper and torn fabric. Bind the strips together with raffia, at a point about five centimetres down the tail. Attach the tails with safety-pins.

The Footmen

The mice who become footmen could wear paper wigs (see *The Footman*) on the previous page.

The Mice

Grey, brown or black leggings, tights and tops would be suitable for the mice costumes. Their long tails can be made in the same way as for the cat, using stockings rather than pop socks. Attach the tails with safety pins, so that they are easily removable.

The children playing mice might like to make their own masks using this template. Cut out the shape and fold along the dotted lines. Bend the ears forward and staple the long strips together. The mask should sit on the top of the head, rather than cover the child's face. Attach elastic to go under the chin and add pipe cleaner whiskers.

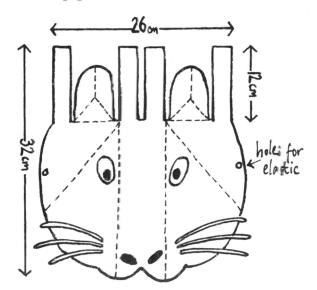

Grabber the Cat

Grabber requires black leggings or tights and a black leotard or long-sleeved top. His tail can be made by stuffing a black nylon pop sock with shredded paper and tying a knot at the top of the sock. His tail should be sewn on. His whiskers can be drawn on with face paints!

Music

You may have a keen, musical member of staff who is prepared to write songs for the play. If not, there are three simple songs included with the play, written to accompany well-known tunes. You will find the words of these songs within the playscript. However, you might like to use songs that the children are already familiar with or to invent your own words.

Some of the actors will be required to sing (while remaining in character). However, it is always a good idea to have a choir leading the songs. The choir involves a great number of children and takes the pressure off the actors, who may be nervous about singing solo.

The songs can be accompanied by piano or guitar, or the school orchestra (if you have one). If not, simple tuned or untuned percussion will work well too.

Dances

There is only one dance called for in the script, and that occurs during Act 2, scene 2, at the ball. Classical music (recorded) is suggested here, unless you want to involve the school orchestra. You may plump for a traditional waltz, or you could present the entire scene as a disco!

You can certainly introduce some more dances into the performance, which gives you the chance to involve a greater number of children, and keeps the audience spellbound during scene changes. For example, you could introduce a woodland animal dance between Act 1, scene 2 and Act 1, scene 3.

Sound Effects

There should be music playing in the background during Act 2, scene 2 (Having a Ball!). Classical music, or a waltz, would be suitable.

You can achieve the sound effects in various ways, but here are some suggestions:

> The approach of Grabber = a drum roll
>
> Thunder rumbling = rattle sheets of flexible cardboard
>
> A thunderclap = a clash of cymbals
>
> A hunting horn = blow a kazoo
>
> A knock at the door = rap a block of wood on a table top
>
> A fanfare = two or three kazoos
>
> A clock striking midnight = twelve strikes on a cymbal
>
> A drum roll = two drums played simultaneously

Anything Else?

Keep calm, and keep smiling! Remember that a poor dress rehearsal always leads to a great performance. Children always rise to the occasion and it's bound to be all right on the night!